My Soul is Bleeding Poetic Whispers

SHANTERIA "POETIZER" GRIGLEN

My Soul is Bleeding – Poetic Whispers
Copyright © 2018 by Poetizer Productions. All rights reserved.

No part of this publication may be reproduced, stored in retrieval system or transmitted in any way by any means, electronic, mechanical, photocopy, recording or otherwise without the prior permission of the author except as provided by USA copyright law.

Poetizer Productions is committed to authentic excellence.

www.poetizerproductions.com

Cover design by Melvin McClanahan

Published in the United States of America

ISBN-10: 0692145362
ISBN-13: 9780692145364

You noticed
My discomfort
And permitted me
To live
Unapologetically.

"Mommy, just be you!"

Those words
Changed my life
To my daughter/best friend
Thank you
For loving me
Unconditionally!

You understand
Our most complicated truths
Those grey areas we tend to erase.

You forgive
The unforgivable
Wrong deeds, done on purpose.

You know
Us to the core of our being
Our flaws don't surprise you.

You bless
Our selfish behaviors
Over and over again
Knowing we don't deserve it.

You love us...still
Even when we don't have the courage
To love ourselves.

You heal
Broken vessels
Using every fracture
To build our stories.

Thank You, Jesus!

CONTENTS

Acknowledgments viii

Introduction 1
The Dawn 3
The Examination 18
The Conviction 34
The Adoration 62
The Refinery 89

In Closing 115

ACKNOWLEDGMENTS

For most of my life, I drowned my ears with noise afraid of the cries within my soul. It was You comforting me when I didn't think I deserved to be loved based on the opinions of others who caused me to question our relationship. Many will never understand my love for You because it looks different, but You complete me. I found wholeness in Your love. You have been my everything when I felt like I had nothing or no one in my life. Without You I would be a blur lost, confused and empty. So, with total admiration I say I love You God and thank You for thinking enough of jacked up me to send Your Son and allow His soul to bleed just so that I would be able to live this life you gave me fearlessly.

How can I not mention you Ms. DuVonne T. Moore, a special thank you for your timeless efforts in assisting me to get this project done. I am beyond grateful for your love and patience. To have you on my team and in my corner is a constant reminder that I'm winning!

To my Mom and Dad, I forgive you and my prayer is that you have forgiven yourselves. This road to forgiveness wasn't easy, but it has been one of my greatest teachers. Thank you for the journey and remember that it all worked out for my good. I love you both dearly!

INTRODUCTION

I pride myself on being able to function through adversity, but the truth is, at times I get tired of being strong. And sometimes I want to break down and cry, but I don't. Instead, I just pack up my feelings and leave them in the shower. A place that knows me intimately, the emotional me, the me that denies My Soul is Bleeding.

Oftentimes we don't recognize we're hurting, but the pain gradually reveals itself through our behaviors. One of the saddest stories is when a person is broken, yet too distracted to acknowledge the dysfunction. 'My Soul is Bleeding' is a poetic, soul-stirring journey that chronicles raw truth which unveils love, guilt, shame, lies, and captures the essence of faith.

This poetic diary will inspire and liberate you to walk in your truth boldly, realizing that your life is not an accident, but a unique journey that must filter out purpose. It is a book for all regardless of age, race, gender or orientation because everyone's soul bleeds. You can survive life after death, but you must be willing to endure the process of being broken.

The Dawn

Genesis 1:1-5 (KJV)

In the beginning, God created the heaven and the earth. And the earth was without form and void, and darkness was upon the face of the deep. And the Spirit of God moved upon the face of the waters. And God said, Let there be light: and there was light. And God saw the light, that it was good: and God divided the light from the darkness. And God called the light Day, and the darkness he called Night. And the evening and the morning were the first day.

Who am I?

That You
Would die for me.

Who am I?

That You
Would bless me
With such vision and creativity.

Who am I?

That I'm chosen
An idea
Created by You
The mind of God.

Once Upon a Time...

On the ninth inning
A child was born
Kicking and screaming
Weighing unbalanced scales
Innocent magic
Forced to take her place
In an unstable world
Born on accident
She wasn't planned
But there was a plan
Pain and purpose
As she began to teeth
My Soul is Bleeding
God's creation
A little giant
The voice of nations
Now a grown woman
Fighting to hide
That little girl
On the inside
Rebellious in nature
Tired of being strong
I'm territorial
Because I want to heal
My Soul is Bleeding
Secret relationships
Made me whole
Love and affection
Stepped in for rejection
A truth teller
Comfortable living a lie
My self-esteem
Isn't high
Cloudy questions
Will I ever be
Completely free
To be the real me?

That Little Girl on The Inside

Oops...
I've arrived
Staring darkness in the eyes
I'm innocent
Wrapped in rejection
Held by judgment
I made no reservations
Fate set this date
A living sacrifice
Competing for parental time
Priorities robbed them blind
I'm a product of sin
Blame my faultless parents
Too young to know better
Dangling in an unfamiliar world
Modern-day Adam and Eve
Biting into a future
Disregarding the importance of me
Without my consent
Regret would haunt them later
What goes around
Has to meet its starting point
Again
I'm paying for sins
That had nothing to do with me
Move out the way
I want to dream
Broken pieces away
She's running
Every step forward
Leads through mess
Too empty to acknowledge the test
Trying to connect the dots

But—
The lessons are hard to learn
Her explanations are wrong
Destiny can't be respected
Surrounded by neglect
Little girl you are free
To scream

You don't have to hide
On the inside any longer
The muzzle has been removed
Don't be confused
Search for the truth
It will set you free
Believe the voice
Within your soul
He wants to make you whole
You've been looking for a way to escape
Wisdom will help you understand fate
Don't ignore destiny
It will introduce you to true purpose
You're not happy
I know
But peace will be planted
As you grow
The tree of life
Has your named engraved
Even though life doesn't always behave
God always has the last say
Let that little girl in you breathe
She wants freedom
From this inner enemy.

Our Souls are Bleeding

There's brokenness in the atmosphere
Creating a multitude of liars and lost sheep
The air is polluted with false inspiration
Desperate for validation
The debris has formed cracks in our minds
Which are now becoming open sores
That have taken our identity
We've been chastised by insecurities
Too hard to be soft, ego vs. pride
A battle we lose daily
Everybody wants to be a boss
Going nowhere
With a crowd of haters
The blood no longer runs warm
In our veins
It's been vexed by shame
Patience isn't a virtue
It's aggravation on steroids
Nobody wants to make the sacrifice
To heal
Social media is our therapy
Just invite broken souls
One after another
Put a band-aid over the root
Of our problems
Nobody wants to admit
That their smile is fake
Simply because we haven't
Forgiven ourselves
For past mistakes
Winning is achieved
But not authentically
As our souls
Are constantly bleeding.

Every Crown has a Cross

I was sick
Not physically

But—
Emotionally numb
Unable to process
This broken record
Expecting things
From seeds I didn't plant
I would feel, but I wasn't feeling
Some called me immature
I say I wasn't groomed
Toxic environments
Don't nurture sensitive emotions
So now there's a mold
An outer exterior that's hard
Inauthentic and selfish
A monster in the making
Doing life with a good heart
And misplaced feelings
Unable to be valued
Because my worth
Was left in my father's semen
And my mother's hips
Neglected before I was born
Too young to know better
So I carried their sins
With shame and a smile
My timing was off
A good heart
Corrupted by worthlessness
So as an adult, I'm selfish
Eager to invite people in
But slow to heal old wounds
I didn't realize
Something was wrong with me
I needed emotional therapy
As a child, my parents' love avoided me.

Poison

Toxic words crippled my emotions
My brain broke down
"people"
Wanted me to believe
Jesus died in vain
"people"
Controlled me with judgment
"people"
Said He wouldn't find my name
In the book of life
"people"
Thought my life was too shameful
Screwed and confused
"people"
Made me a hostile witness
Within myself
Afraid to be honest
"people"
Made me proud
To sleep with lies
Bleeding internally
But "people"
Didn't win.
God came and rescued me
Showed me what I needed
To know
Now that sinner
Plants stories into others
And watch them grow
So, to ALL those
"people"
Who raped my conscience
This cheer is for you
Middle finger in the air
Yes, this was about you!

Leave Me Alone

I had the audacity
To walk through my pain
By myself
Spirit and truth
Fighting for freedom
On a daily basis
And every step I took
Hurt like hell
I felt the rawness in my brokenness
Scattered and torn
Laid out for the world to see
Stop talking about me
You have no idea
What it takes to be me
Diseased by neglect
Scarred by a permanent hole
Secretly living in my chest
Too deep to confess
It pierced my flesh
Until I told the truth
It hurt like hell
But it freed me
Now you can understand
Why my soul was bleeding.

Born to Hurt

While in my mother's womb
I was being groomed by sin
Unfaithful sperm captured my emotions
Swimming in polluted water
Too tainted to breathe positive energy
Not understanding love
Would be my future malfunction
My path was already created
There was no turning back
When my infant body saw the light of day
I became a slave to a misbehaved world
Filled with tears and responsibility
Which left me seeking satisfaction
In all the wrong places
I was deaf to beauty
Unimportant and being molested
Would be my claim to fame
No one can help a silent child
Life was too busy to pay attention
I played thoughts, pen and paper
Like a guitar hero
We had unprotected sex all the time
The silhouette convicts my human nature
A profound weakness
Turned into greatness
I'm loyal to my past
Although it kicked me in my ass
It prepared me to be a spoken vessel
For a nation
That can no longer ignore me
You see
God was equipping me
With fierce testimonies
Silence is not my language
Fear doesn't control me anymore
I speak the truth
My sacrifice is being judged
A saved sinner
With a story
Chasing a purpose
Which passes all understanding.

Damaged Goods

I'm running naked
Carefree and unattached
What you see
Is not the proper version
The authentic
Has been erased
The residue
Long lines of confusion
Carrying the burden
Tainted by neglect
First class selfishness
Seated on a one-way street
Misunderstood brick roads
Guide me in the wrong direction
Too far gone to turn around
Along the way
I cherish part-time satisfaction
Consumed by the moments
Too scarred to believe
In a positive future
A created character
Defines my lifestyle
Happiness ignores my presence
Temporary satisfaction excites me
I have a private life
That seeks public attention
It's intriguing to regular species
But for me
A toxic disease
Spectacle 24 hours a day
Everybody has something to say
But has anyone prayed
For a battered soul
Waiting to be rescued
From a cult that influences
My sinful nature
Dreaming of the day
Real life can step out the closet.

It Was Back Then

If you asked me what was wrong
I'd say nothing
Only because I can't express it with words
Here, hold my heart in your hands
Go ahead, apply more pressure
Get to the core of me
Maybe you'll feel the inadequate beats
Don't be afraid
It's just blood
The Creator's form of love
I've been instructed to tell the truth
So, let it run into your pores
My emotions secretly live all over the place
But I've trained them on how to behave
Trying to escape the wind of understanding
One second, I'm up
The next minute I'm down
With no real explanation
Because
Nothing's wrong right now
It was back then
That has my mind misinterpreted
Searching for an answer
To expose what I feel
I'm always real
Maybe just not with myself
A grown woman externally
An oversized baby internally
Emotionally I'm in pampers
How could this be me? Easy
You see I was born into confusion
Mixed with guilt, tears and pain
The truth had to be my guardian
So, I was parentless for years
Searching high and low
Still couldn't find nobody
I just wanted to be raised
Not tolerated as an inconvenience
It was back then
That had my emotions
Misinterpreted.

Bruised but Not Broken

How could the one
Who treated you cold
Warm your heart
The two that
Vandalized your emotions
Touch a place
That many ignore
The three that
Wanted friendship
Just to escape stability
The four that
Said we're better apart
To avoid the stress
The five that
Unknowingly lied
But-
In spite of it all
You got through it
Pain didn't win
Courage allowed you
To embrace ignorant behaviors
On purpose
You may be limping
But you're also fearless
Powerful magic
That old grass
Wasn't so green
You're spending time
With self
Becoming great
Manifesting miracles
Through past mistakes.

Family Secrets

Generation after generation
Blood becomes thicker than truth
Sweep what hurts under the rug
Allow the dust to form piles in empty spaces
Make sure the family name stays clean
Even if the emotional residue feels dirty
Pretend HE didn't touch you, and SHE was just being nurturing
It's okay because you know these strangers
They're the keys to your childhood scars
But no one will ever know
Because you won't muster a word
The day after has now turned into decades later
Time has passed, but the pain is as fresh as an open wound
Not only are you scarred
But your brain has been washed with lies
Just forgive them and move on
It happened so long ago
After all, it's your fault
You should have said something back then
When you were innocent
And being physically and emotionally manipulated
Family secrets turn little girls and boys
Into adult slaves
Groomed to protect the residue
Keep it tucked away
Until the anger manifests itself
Toward a person of choice
And not the person of interest
You're frustrated because that secret
Is secretly eating at the core of your happiness
Silence is not golden - it's toxic
Now you have your own child and you're overprotective
Everybody is a suspect
You feel like the curse is broken
And your secrets are comfortable
You didn't put family on your watch list
Now your child has to deal with this generational BS!
"Me too" has become a trend in our family's roots
All because we struggle
With the burden and battle
Of not being able to expose ugly family truths.

The Examination

Jeremiah 4:19 (NIV)

Oh, my anguish, my anguish!
  I writhe in pain.
Oh, the agony of my heart!
  My heart pounds within me,
  I cannot keep silent.
For I have heard the sound of the trumpet;
  I have heard the battle cry.

It can take a lifetime
To heal a pain
That was created
In a moment…

Insecure

You found me
Headstrong
Focused on a dream
Picture perfect
Ideal candidate
Putting pieces together
One brick at a time
Mind over matter
I needed to purge
But you were beautiful
I wasn't ready
But you were different
I prayed for you
But I wasn't groomed properly
A life-long battle
Bruised and broken
Attraction hid my flaws
What you saw
Sparked your interest
And instantly
Desire took over
Breathing with shattered lungs
Engulfed in flames
That would one day
Burn us to a crisp
Distracted by newness
Red flags looked green
Go with the flow
But we don't really know
Each other
Hidden cameras
Invisible hearts
Emotionally immature
Scarred by past mistakes
Licking our wounds along the way
Beautiful souls
Tired and unsure
But we kept on going
Smiling through the process
Until nighttime
Our reflections are dark

Secrets unknown
Magnetic energy
Yet, we can't see
Each other's inner selves
A place that hasn't healed
Under construction
Love has intercepted
The pain
We build in spite of
Lost and insecure
Years later
Toxic chemistry exposed
Our connection
Is on life support
Blurred vision
We can't find
Our reason
Distance reveals wisdom
I see my errors
But now your heart
Is too damaged
Forgiveness gets a thumbs down
My insecurities
Left you
Emotionally numb.

Karma Reloaded

What goes around comes around
Chants from a broken heart
Blah... blah... blah...
A figment of their imagination
Caused by me
Too prideful
So I bend corners
Avoiding the truth
My coast is clear
Years have passed
Old wounds have been patched
No more guilty monkeys
Jumping on my back.
This new life has me grateful
Loyal and faithful
I'm not the person I used to be
I am free from sin's penalties
Payback is the farthest thing from my mind
I've had time to grow
You can't punish me for things I didn't know
But what if I did
Know better
And didn't do better
Ego at its finest
Camouflaged mistakes
Viewed as life lessons
Courage to move forward
Neglecting the possibilities
Of that old karma
Coming to deal with me
Blah...blah...blah...
I've been forgiven
Permission to embrace a better life
One that doesn't take
A heart for granted on purpose
Thank God for Jesus, He saved me
I've made a conscious decision
To walk with freedom daily
Life has come full circle
Things are falling into place
Even those old selfish mistakes

As I'm experiencing my happy ever after
But, I'm not happy
Everything seems perfect
So I don't understand the dilemma
My heart is confused
Blah...blah...blah...
Getting what I want
But lacking what I need
Life is doing to me
What I've done to others
It's coming closer
Too hard to bear
I want out
But karma won't let me go
I have to sit in it faithfully
Feel the tears of many years ago
Going in circles
Dangerous peace
Keeps me on my knees
All because karma had to be free
To torment me
Not as punishment
But as a tool
I needed to know how they felt
That way, I wouldn't ever
Hurt somebody else
On purpose
Forced focus
Karma reloaded!

I Hate You...

You neglected me
So, I should hate you, but I don't
Being abandoned taught me how to survive.
I want to hate you, but I can't
You made me despise myself
I should hate you, but I don't
Self-hatred gave me a reason to hope.
I want to hate you, but I can't
You raped me
I should hate you, but I don't
That assault perfected my need for God.
I want to hate you, but I can't
You kept me in bondage
I should hate you, but I don't
Being in bondage made me an answer.
I want to hate you, but I can't
You lied to me
I should hate you, but I don't
Those lies made me more aware.
I want to hate you, but I can't
You took my innocence
I should hate you, but I don't
Violating my innocence taught me how to be strong
I want to hate you, but I can't
You crushed me
I should hate you, but I don't
That crushing produced oil.
I want to hate you, but I can't
God doesn't hate me
I should hate you, but I don't
Affliction was necessary
Pain
I want to hate you, but I can't
You infused my purpose.

He Told Me Not to Tell

Have you ever needed an answer that didn't want to be questioned?

Why did he pick me? Was it because I was pretty? Did he really care about me? Whatever the answer, I was a little girl too young for the attention.

This isn't right, but I never said no until the last time. There I was in an off-white slip with a black rubber hammer in my hand, don't touch me anymore or I'm going to tell Mama!

His touch didn't hurt me physically; it just crippled me mentally. An emotional trauma that poisoned my life and caused me to blossom into a whirlwind of carelessness.

You would think that I was currently living in my childhood by the way I'm able to vividly describe to you how it has failed me in my adult life.

I've spent so much time doubting who I am and my credibility as a girl. I grew up hiding behind layers of clothes not because I was trying to be cool, but I didn't want anyone to notice me. If you noticed me, that meant you could possibly hurt me just like he did.

All this stemmed from your need to satisfy your desires, a desire that snatched my pretty away.

You opened a door that blinded my innocence and stripped me of the beauty of sex.

I grew up giving myself away because you touched me; not with love, but perversion.

I'm giving you your flowers while you're still alive; it wasn't a mistake, the pain you caused me made me great.

It's a part of my story, and God gets all the glory!

Her Voice...

Can I have your attention
Wait I already have that
You gaze at my actions
But let me explain
I'm a poster child
For unresolved pain
Don't whisper
Or judge
My unhealthy
Behaviors
I need to clarify some things
You aren't my real friends
I know
But you have helped
To grow this monkey
Riding on my back
My behavior isn't me
Well, it is but it isn't
You laugh and smile
Making me parade
More
I show
More
I act out of character
Often
Nobody checks
Because
Nobody cares
I'm your entertainment
The truth is
I'm loud
Because
I'm actually afraid
My smiles
Aren't real
I make you laugh
Because
I'm not happy
You won't ever
See my tears
I don't want to deal

With the frowns
Yes
I'm defensive
Boldness protects me
You see life
Plucked me when
I wasn't looking
Now every eye I see
Wants things I can't give
I'm broken
If you knew the real me
You'd judge
Sex sells
It's my daily inspiration
It's the only way
You'll pay
Me some attention
Everybody is known
For something
Freak fits me well
I don't like the title
But
It tickles
Many minds
Or maybe not
I have no real substance
No real threat
Stereotype defines me
Foreign to my purpose
So I lose focus
Attracting the wrong attention
My name holds no value
Just honorable mentions
Who I am is very important
But you'll never know it
I sleep with my eyes open
Brokenness wrote this.

Thorn in My Side

A beautiful branch
Stuck in between my flesh
I personally put it in an improper zone
Forgetting about the consequence
Enjoying the pleasure
Now I am bleeding
Exhausted by the roller coaster ride
No more butterflies
Too weak to flap their wings
Leaving a sad cocoon
Embarrassed
So, I can't complain
I'm the cause
Of my own pain
Dancing with another insecurity
I've become negative
Lost in pride
Rotating this thorn in my side.

Slutty Emotions

I've prostituted my emotions
They are naked
Laying in different hearts
Torn and worn out
Starting from the crown of my head
Finishing at the heels of my feet
Free of charge
Exposed for the world to see
Just enjoying the moment
Avoiding future consequences
Angelic lies blind my sight
I'm single
Too broken to mingle
But no one notices
Until it's too late
I've infected your heart
With my charismatic charm
Enticing looks and spoken words
A bowl of bacteria
Poisoning those who seek
Unconditional acceptance
Anticipating fulfillment
But receiving temporary satisfaction
Always leading me back
To point A, B, and C
A place I should have stayed
But no
My heart won't rest
Until it has beat down every challenge
Or maybe its every victim
That yearns for emotional validation
Too selfish to care about the sacrifice
Just make the mood mellow and work a wonder
Love is what I want to feel
But it's not an emotion
I'm willing to give
Not because I'm cold blooded
But
My blood is cold.

I Almost Fell

I almost fell
Into temptation
Eyes spoke the truth
Lies made sense
Chemistry under the influence
You and me
Seeing each other
For the first time
Let's go half
On a good feeling
Making it memorable
Never forget
Go crazy
But wait
What about her
At home
In another city
Trusting you completely
While on vacation
You want me
Spring break fantasy
Years of one day
Ready for display
Opportunity has knocked
And lust wants to bite me
I'm bickering with karma
What goes around
Might come
At the right time
Wrong person
Paying for a mistake
I needed to make
I almost fell
Into temptation.

I'm Not Crazy

Every time I turn around
I bump into false relationships
Little hope with huge let downs
Family and friends
Betray me unknowingly
I'm tired of being let down
Looked over
Pushed to the side and left for dead
How can I be the life of the party
When I'm not even living?
I sleepwalk through my days
Praying for a better way
I can't see
My mind controls me
I've avoided liberty
For the comfort of never being alone
Being wronged haunts my emotions
Constant failures beat on me
My brain refuses to shut up
It's hard being human
Laughter is expected anytime I'm around
What's wrong is shouted out loud
Anytime I'm not performing my routine smile
I'm not allowed to have a bad day
Friends pull on me for energy
Even when I'm empty
I need help
But wouldn't that mean
I'm crazy
Just like everybody else.

Invisible Tears

This wound is fresh
So the pain
Won't come until later
During the healing process
We've been in this place
On several occasions
Bumps and bruises
Keeps us stagnant
Walking in the dark
Committed to making it work
Even if we're not happy
Celebrity status
If only they knew
Our truth
Invisible tears
All over the place
Cup running over
Seeping through layers
Of unresolved pain
It's not as bad
As it feels
But the disconnect
Is deadly
We're starving for answers
Love isn't enough
Abandoned by affection
Our reality has become
Daily rejection unknowingly
Now we're marching
Through April showers
Afraid that as a couple
We've lost our power
Not because our love isn't real
There's just too many
Invisible tears.

The Conviction

Psalm 51:3 (KJV)

For I acknowledge my transgressions: and my sin is ever before me.

I have a disease that's toxic-friendly
No matter what I do it wears me like a suit
It pierces my flesh daily
External perfection at its best
Inside a mental mess
I like to call it a serial rapist
Violating my thoughts
Constantly fighting my conscience
Unprotected emotions
Being exposed
Breakfast, lunch and dinner
What am I?
Bona fide sinner!

Truth Is...

I'm not as strong
As I appear to be
Courageous, but weak
Every day is a fight
The mind
Is a terrible thing to waste
So I feed it
By being productive
Praying and listening
For God's next move
And still
My mind and spirit
Battle for permission
To rule my day
Between what I
See, feel and know
In this place
Unwanted conversations
About faults, failures and future
It's this dark voice
That makes me question
Everything I do
Am I good enough?
Is my living in vain?
Will I ever be
More than my sexuality?
Because that's the focus
The message is constantly missed
A wounded healer
Encouraging everyone else
Except me.

Porn Star

There was a time when I could count on one...maybe two hands, the soul ties that made it into my record book.
But now, those numbers are faint and plenty.
Many strangers felt kin to me because my body was toxic-friendly.
Being with someone you want but don't need is the exact definition of sleeping with the enemy.
I used to be ashamed, but I've learned that repetitive, meaningless sex is a scar from unresolved pain.
There's a consequence for being molested or introduced to sex prematurely; you don't value the intimacy because the experience has been tainted.
As the years passed, attention became an idol. I used it as fuel to fill in gaps I didn't know existed until adulthood.
I was ignorant to the weight of sex; it meant little-to-nothing to me. All I wanted was for this void on the inside of me to go away.
So over and over and over again, time after time, I'd play with my demons and came out of the situation empty every time.
My cravings were unhealthy and left me worse than when I started.
No matter how cute, pretty or attractive they were - I was always left incomplete.
But then I met a Man. One who not only touched me but held my pain in the palms of His hands.
He touched me with His blood and washed all my sins away.
Oh yes, He touched me like I've never been touched before! This peaceful touch left me whole; a new sense of worth.
The Blood, God, Jesus...whatever you want to call Him works!
I have never had such loyalty - my body is finally at peace and not in pieces.
Intimacy with God was the greatest intercourse I've ever experienced.
I pray you find liberty in this misdiagnosed truth.
The truth is - being low is a process that helps us to get high spiritually.
It's a route we often take for God to straighten out the messes that life has made.

Consequential Selfishness

On the outside looking in
A mature woman
Marinated with wisdom
From the inside out
A foolish girl
Influenced by selfishness
What I've done
Is unforgivable
Physically adopted a habit
That emotionally destroyed a soul
Playing with temporary
Stained by lifelong injuries
Inviting this secret torch
Into every heart I meet
I've done what I did
Now happy feet
Are paralyzed by neglect
I'm empty
Meaning there's nothing left
For me to give
But regret
A new label now reads
"Getting close to me
Could be a threat"
Haunted by consequential selfishness.

Envious

Oh, how sweet it must be
To taste the freedom
In being opposite of me
Walking with your head held high
Released from this prison
No longer incarcerated
By self-hate or unworthiness
True example of God's power
First-class recommendation
Religion wants the world to see
If He did it for you
Then surely
He can do it for those like me
No more hiding
Being in the closet
Is no longer your home
Deliverance has found your name
You can smile now
Everyone is applauding
Acceptance is your new best friend
Beauty of the beast
While defeat beats up on me
My insides tremble
That's what they want to see
Happen to me, but
I prayed that same prayer
Kept my mind on Him
Turned around seven times
Shook the devil off
Turned from my wicked ways
Fast and prayed some more
And I even tried to hate the sin
But there I was
Doing it again
And again
Feeling sorry
Yet again
Why won't it leave me ?
Devil move out the way
I want to be free
Why won't God deliver me?

You get to walk in the royal court
While I dance with slaves
A world that hates my sexuality
Before they even get to know me
Marked as damaged goods
I'm not an evil person
And for the record
The devil isn't my master
I actually love God
So stop it!
I'm not going to hell!
This thorn
Hurts at times
I have to fight to be me
Because unlike you
He didn't deliver me
Envy...

Death to Depression

Like a blind bullet
Causality of circumstance
Hit by a stray spirit
Eager to kill, steal and destroy
The audacity of hope
Standing on the ledge
Ready to visit the Creator
Not on schedule
But ahead of time
Your mind is tired
Fighting is how you breathe
Bruised and bloody knees
No one can see your enemy
Invisible shame
Afraid to be called crazy
This curse
Haunts you daily
You want to live
But your worth doesn't add up
Nothing has changed
It seems to be getting worse
So death sounds appealing
Once you're gone
Peace will finally be still
No more tears to cry
Controlling your destiny
Forgetting those who are invested
In your future
You just need the pain to stop
But it recycles itself
Over and over again
Confusion that's hard to explain
No matter what you do
It won't go away
Russian roulette
Maybe tonight
You'll take your life
Make all the wrong things right
Perception is winning
Every ambition, goal and dream
Defeated and silenced

You missed your mark
Wasted too much time
Set up by your inner me
Mind, body and soul
Day after day
Insanity won't let you pray
Desert prayers
Fatigue and hopeless
Suicide wrote this
You're free
But you didn't die
The blood was running
Warm in your veins
An angel came
Whispered in your ear
Reminded you of your dim light
And how powerful it was
So you gave life
One more try
Hallelujah
You're free
You didn't die
Pushing through the flaws
A heavy cross to bear
But you're still here
Amongst the living
Still breathing
Life's burdens
With stronger lungs
You've been revived
By the Holy Son.

Internal Truth

On the inside
I cry
At least once a day
Dodging stones
That want my attention
On the outside
I smile
Sparkling wisdom
But how
Can I
Encourage
Somebody else!
The valley I'm sneaking through
Is screaming out
For help
The sound of silence
Is loud
Wise words
Makes my thought of the day
Anointed and profound
But I'm no different
Than you
I need Him too
Respect my truth
Uncertainties don't avoid me
Dreams taunt my patience
At times I feel alone
I don't always have an answer
Sometimes I enjoy doing the wrong thing
I'm human
With a slight twist
Be strong
Let God fight your battles
I feel like a snake
With a dislocated rattle
Infectious words
Can quench one's thirst

But——
That doesn't exclude
The poison from being hurt…

Domestic Love

If he ever puts his hands on you...
LEAVE
A saying I've heard a million times
But my heart found it hard to believe
This boy loves me
Although it hurts
I've never had a love like this
One that hits me for being attractive
Maybe it's my fault, I should have listened
A broken pattern threaded into my soul
Love had manipulated my common sense
It told me that his violent nature symbolized
Commitment, loyalty, and devotion
But the giant in me couldn't fully submit
Yet, I'd endure another hit
I didn't think it was that bad
Until I saw my future
This couldn't be the life for me
God, I need Thee
My eyes were blinded by his affection and power
A beautiful beast camouflaged with a smile
Victim of circumstance
Childhood demons held him captive
Hitting me was his release
Until enough was too much and I couldn't endure the pain
Something had to change
I found the strength to call on the name
That's above any other name
God was my only hope
To redeem my broken pieces
Why did I think I could do it alone?
The devil wanted me to think I was alone
But he was a liar
I had to remove the mask in order to escape
Faking it wasn't working
God wanted my truth
I had to plead my case
He turned my suffering into a testimony
Brought me to a powerful place
That introduced me to His prominent grace.

Dear Church Folks...

You lied
God never hated me
It was you
Being uncomfortable with my truth
I wasn't clean in your sight
I'm that neighbor you're supposed to love
But my flesh is hard to digest
Lusting after details about who I sleep with at night
Shame on you wanting to know
Yet you disregard this hole in my soul
Casting me to hell
Too religious to see
Hell is here on earth with you
Every Sunday
Judging me for walking in my truth
When all I need
Is a word to keep me from falling
Into death's hands
Did you pray?
No, you whispered
And missed your assignment
To love on God's child
My biggest distraction
Is I love God
And
I'm gay
It's hard to see the Christ in me
But I promise
My heart is pure
Not only did you lie to me
But you lied to you
You thought you were better
Just look in the mirror
His blood wasn't just for me
Your rumors are true
Secret sins
Need Jesus too
You lied
God never hated me
It was you!

Who Am I?

I looked in the mirror
The reflection I saw
A saved sinner
With good intentions
Looking into eyes
That constantly hurt
Lovable souls
Engulfed in a habit
That has diluted itself
Into my daily struggle
If my heart had a voice
It would say...
I'm not comfortable
In this skin
What's wrong with me?
I know better

But—
Doing better
Is distant
Put me on the cross
To die
Crucify my malfunctions
Then in three days
Bring me back
To a new life
A place where
Faults don't exist
And Eve
Didn't bite
The forbidden fruit
That unlocked
A woman's misery
I am
My own enemy.

The Reality of My Sexuality

Tears are universal
That's what my sorrow sings
Convictions are seasoned
That's what my soul has witnessed
Sins are unleashed
That's what the preacher preached
God's laws must be obeyed
That's what the Bible says
So my faith
Has made my reality
A slave
Held hostage
In a society
That throws stones
At my misunderstood sexuality
So, what do I do
Outside of being confused?
I hide behind the obvious
I lie about the truth
I ask God what He wants me to do
I cry within my laughter
I deny the rumors
I suppress the desires
I cast myself into the fire
I think positive through others
I protect secret lovers
I try to fix the brokenness
I flirt with hope
I pray for it to go away
But everyday
I'm face-to-face
With a beast
That haunts me
There's always a word
That tries to correct my fate
But I'm in an empty room
With a loud audience
Waiting for me to speak
As I step to the microphone
My voice is silenced
The swag I've embodied

Speaks for my identity
I let whispers flow
Pretending not to know
What's being said
I'm not stupid
I just play dumb
Discernment is my friend
So, pretending
Is a form of me being ignorant
It's my belief in God
That makes this road hard
My faith is uncomfortable
Being who I feel like I am
Religion stones me to death
Unaware of my purpose
But you can't see
I've connected with my spirituality
Which reminds me that
I'm still Gods child
When friends and family judge me
God still loves me
Have mercy on people like me
Because you don't know
What they go through
To battle with an identity
That makes their sexuality a reality.

Suicide

Standing on a ledge
Contemplating this jump
Look up
There's a blue sky
Too high to reach
Look down
Every mistake
Is waiting for your fall
The ground is cheering
Jump...jump...jump!
Into self-pity
A blazing furnace
Parading with the living dead
A place where fear
Rules insecurities
With doubt and unbelief
Nobody cares about your dreams
They will never...ever...
Come true
It's a waste of time
Come join us
In the pavement
Of hopelessness
No one will notice
That you are gone
You gave up
On the unknown
Because
You couldn't see
A fulfilled destiny
The spirit in you
Should have waited
A little longer
Patience is the key
You would have
Seen God's glory
Provision for the vision
You could have
Lived out your dreams
Closing the chapter
On make believe

Putting enemies
Under your feet
If only faith had priority
Over friends and family
You would have made it
A sturdy ladder
To reach a blue sky
That seemed impossible
The journey
Never easy
But worth the sacrifice
Ordered steps can't jump
They must be guided
Into purpose
And blinded
By distractions
Shadowing the favor
Of God's grace.

Why

Why did You create me?
Why do I have these feelings?
Why do I have to always explain it?
Why do I hate myself?
Why can't I be free?
Why don't people understand?
Why won't You change me?
Why does my heart beat for him/her?
Why does my family/friends talk about me behind my back?
Why do I have to lie about the truth?
Why are Christians so judgmental?
Why do people think I don't have a relationship with You?
Why am I such a horrible person?
Why isn't Your grace sufficient for me?
Why do people want me to believe that You hate me?
Why won't You answer this prayer?
Why am I gay?

Abort the Mission

Fresh out of high school
Focused on a dream
That was too immature
To come true
I was filled with poison
Searching for a remedy
To secure
My vulnerability
In the beginning
He was the answer
Cute and funny
A combination
Too divine
Yet
Toward the end
He became the problem
My infection
A sore
Oozing with stupidity
Laugh now, cry later
Became his weapon
Of choice
Unprotected sex
At its finest
God...
Please don't
Let a baby
Transpire inside
My womb
Time and time again
I'd escaped
The bullet
Until I got
Brainwashed
Thinking
I was invisible
Because I'm always
Careful
Now I'm the statistic
A young black girl
Having sex

Without respect
That baby
I prayed not to exist
Has entered into
An unwanted place
What will you do?
Was my mother's question
Fear took over
The decision
Was made through
My mother's desires
permission wasn't needed
My voice
Had no conscience
The money was found
I'd experienced
A tragedy
An emotion
Without patience
Ashamed at the outcome
I held myself
In a fetal position
Wishing I could
Take it back
But...
It was too late
The blood
Was on my hands
My heart
Hated me
For the baby
I didn't keep.

Karma

What comes around
Reflects what went around
I did whatever I wanted to do
Never taking into consideration
What I was putting someone's heart through
I've always made my life about me
I didn't have the sense
To learn from a complicated childhood
I carried this infectious disease
Killing any emotion
That gave me the time of day
Intellectual conversation
Served with a cute face and caring heart
Fed my disguise
It gave me conditions to hide behind
A loving person who was mentally malfunctioning
I meant well, but my nurturing abilities
Always failed when it was time to report for duty
Exposing myself or becoming vulnerable
To another's needs
Was a defect
I didn't want to comprehend
Who's going to protect me?
Has always been my theology
There was no time to think about others
Every relationship I encountered
Was paying for the sins of my mother
I'm not making excuses
Just trying to connect
With what I've sown
That way I wouldn't have to reap
The things I've done wrong.

That's Just My Baby Daddy

To watch my daughter silently yearn for the attention of her father breaks my heart because I chose him out of validation, not desire. For years I blamed myself for my selfish decisions - they cost her more than it was worth.

I was unknowingly repeating my mother's old habit, sponsoring my body as a tool to produce a child with a donor who would suddenly withdraw any obligations or responsibility once my womb was stretched to capacity.

My insecurities wanted his cuteness and popularity to upgrade my low self-esteem. I wasn't worthy to be his girlfriend; he was someone I didn't believe I deserved to have, so him having an interest in me was poison.

Out of nowhere, I was the girl wearing his Nautica jacket, stamped with approval, not knowing that his availability wasn't limited to just me. Blinded by his ability to make me laugh, I rejected common sense and embraced the attention.

Honestly, I never thought about if he grew up in a good home, if he was a respectable guy or if he had dreams he wanted to pursue. I just wanted him to pick me; allow *me* to be that special girl. In my defense, I was never taught to seek substance, so his beautiful smile and pretty boy swag were enough for me to accept his invitation.

I lacked confidence and I desired to be attached to anything that would make me believe I was important or of worth.

I remember whispering the idea of having a beautiful child by him to my best friend not knowing that there was power in my tongue and that my causal words would soon become reality.

The laughs were lighter and the fun stopped. He wasn't cute anymore because now, I'm pregnant - fresh out of school! What am I going to do?

Wait, there's another baby by *another* girl? I'm not the only one? How could I have been so stupid? Easy…I wanted him to validate a piece in me that he wasn't qualified to. I was caught up in my feelings and the desire to be loved by a boy even though I knew it was a dead end.

He had failed me, not because he was a bad person, but because he was a broken boy trying to fill in the blanks that left me empty.

I became his victim, another baby mama who didn't take time to see that the cute baby-maker was incapable of being a father.

What was supposed to be my daughter's first love is just a man who helped me to produce an amazing child - thank you baby daddy.

Draw Me Close to You

You must be in heaven shaking your head
At all the perverted things I do and say
It's not easy living this way...
Especially when my transgressions
Have me glued to fear
I say I love You
Yet I act like I don't know how to trust You fully.

I say You're good all the time,
Yet I try to block Your voice out of mind.

I say You're a forgiving God,
Yet I make life for myself so hard.

I say I believe You died on the cross for me,
Yet I refuse to surrender to You completely.

I say You're a keeper,
Yet I live in a camp where the devil is my reaper.

I say I'm saved
Yet I lose control and allow my body to misbehave.

I say I know that everything happens for a reason,
Yet I allow my failures to disqualify me
From being allowed to have rainy seasons.

I know You love me unconditionally,
But I honestly don't feel worthy of such generosity.

Pray the Gay Away

Closets are dark
Shadows of loneliness
Running from reality
Whispers rape your conscience
The bleeding is nonstop
This makes you different
Talking to lies
Trying to be straight
Praying to make it through those gates
Inside you want to change
But things remain the same
A constant battle
With a lifestyle
Too weak to be respected
Fighting to be understood
A walking canvas
Of rejection
The topic that requires the most attention
Castaway is what they say
You can't love God and live like this
Repent ...repent... repent...!
Coming out means
Lights on
To a blinded world
Looking for remedies
To question Gods authority
Why me?
Soaking in misery
Like a fried tomato
Our brains are dull
Crispy Christians
Gasping for air
Speaking religion
Outsourcing spirituality
No nutrition
For healthy hearts
Believers in speech
Haters in soul
No substance to grow
Love can't be shown
Too much politicking

About the levels of sin
YES!
God is disappointed
We all fall short
Missing the mark
Mercy and grace
Can't be replaced
So why be biased
About the things
You don't understand?
Doesn't God
Have the whole world
In His hands?
His love
Surpasses all understanding
There's a different path
For every individual
Our hearts
Tell the real story
Place a mirror
In front of your chest
Now ask the world
What sins do *you* need to confess...?

Tired

My flesh won't let me go
A soul desperate for redemption
My flesh won't let me go
A heart seeking God's faithfulness
My flesh won't let me go.
A made-up mind this time
My flesh won't let me go
I'm tired of being tired
My flesh won't let me go
Yet...
I'm praying for forgiveness
The question
Why me?
The congregation
Filled with worshipping saints
But I
Must wrestle
With a flesh
Of mind and body
That taunts me
About my sins
Not again
I'm sick
Of this!
God
We already talked
I confessed
The pressure was released
But now
It's creeping back in
What do you want
Me to do?
I'm weak
You already know
The circle has changed
I can't see
The outcome
Pain and confusion
Are the headliners
I need You
To love me

Because I'm
Not loving myself
We're not connecting
Give me
Another word
Something to build
Me up
Before I'm
Torn back down
Why me?

The Adoration

1 Peter 4:8 (NLT)

Most important of all, continue to show deep love for each other, for love covers a multitude of sins.

You feel like...
Pain
You taste like...
Hurt
You smell like...
Brokenness
I see...
Love.

Grace Lifted Me

Close the door
It's time to remove the mask
I need to peel off toxic layers
Phony smiles and confused laughter
I'm getting weaker by the day
Death seems like a solution
I don't have the strength to pretend
Society has poisoned my thoughts
People's opinions run through my veins
I live in a tank filled with lies
The air I breathe is desperate
Searching for wholeness
Tired of self-healing
My anxieties keep me restless
Unworthy of love
The pain has left me hopeless
Untainted love
Something that doesn't fade
Beyond my comprehension
Is what my heart desires
A spiritual intimacy
One that lifts the burdens of life
His Words are poetry
They shadow my emotions
When the days are dim
I find grace, love and refuge in Him.

Neither One of Us

Here we are
Stuck between a rock
And a hard place
Smiling and arguing
Losing our religion
About to give up
Faithless and fearful
Day by day
The beauty in our energy
Is rapidly fading away
Once a dream
Now a nightmare
Unsure of our future
A unique chemistry
Losing its flame
Every disagreement creates
New layers of pain
Mountains of hopelessness
It's getting harder to climb
The distance is scary
We don't understand one another
Misguided perceptions
Too distracted to trust our faith
That we're meant to be
Feels like catastrophic hemorrhaging
Let's try one more time
And we're good
Until the next time
Over and over again
Peace won't come in
Freedom is what we crave
Let's just be friends
Pretend love doesn't exist
No more sleepless nights
Manipulate the process
Pushing us to be greater
Than cute pictures

And inspirational sayings
High on our influence
But our relationship
Is on life support
Literally about to die
But neither one of us
Wants to be the first
To say goodbye.

Hopeful

My heart doesn't skip
It jumps when I think about
The possibilities
I'm emotionally ready
To take a chance
On the unknown
So I find myself
Mingling with eagles
Flying through imaginary friends
Trying to scope out
Which wind
Gets you to smile
Your way
Into my life
Future
I don't know the when's or where's
But
I'll be there
Waiting
Anticipating greatness.

I'm the key to my own success
I'm bigger than my failures
I'm the truth outspoken.

Black Girl Magic

We need you like never before
Look at your daughters, nieces, sisters and friends
We can hear the silent sound of hope in the atmosphere
As the complexities of life penetrates our thoughts
The world as a whole is becoming overwhelmed
With the rapid rotation of brokenness
Found in a woman's worth
Every day we battle to exist
In a world that does not value
Our Queenmanship
Beauty is no longer
About how we treat people
Or help others
We are confused
Our biggest flaws-
Being phony, selfish and envious
Of our sisters
Who have put on the breastplate
Of greatness
We don't know how to be happy
For one another
Because life has not shown us
Our best days yet
And the wait is uncomfortable
This darkness is only an echo
We need you to fix our postures
By loving and encouraging us
When we fall
Teach us how to be warring women
We think we know
But have no idea
About the weight of the burden
You've had to carry throughout the years
Mold us into a redefined prototype
That will take advantage
Of the power found
In being a woman
Not just any woman
But, a virtuous woman!

But God…

I was mentally torn but…I made it
I was physically a mess but…I made it
I was spiritually cheating but…I made it
I was psychologically lost but…I made it
I was emotionally disoriented but…I made it
I couldn't see the importance of life but…God!

It was lonely but…I made it
It was difficult but…I made it
It was at times unbearable but…I made it
It was painful but…I made it
It was chaotic but…I made it
It was crippling but…God!

I had to hide my tears but…I made it
I had to let go but…I made it
I had to hurt people's feelings but…I made it
I had to sacrifice but…I made it
I had to endure critics but…I made it
I had to fall flat on my face but…God!

Wishful Thinking

I said I was ready
But, for what?
I'm not sure
Watch and wait
For what?
I'm not sure
Could be a feeling
Emotional healing
Or maybe not
Eyes play tricks
Magical beliefs
In false perceptions
Hoping to encounter
Different blessings
A Martian
From planet you
Floating to the inside
In search of life
Too deep to focus
On outer appearance
Layers of hurt
Need to be confiscated
True love
Secretly hides in shame
Afraid to witness pain
Just open up
TRUST
So potential
Can introduce
Single me to us.

Parking Lot Conversations

Hi...my name is...
Chemistry doesn't lie
Everybody knows
You're beautiful
What they can't see
Is that damaged heart
Still beating, slowly
Just enough
For me to pay attention
Depositing coins of wisdom
Layer after layer
Being swept away
Still a faint pulse
Authentic and pure love
The size of a mustard seed
Bigger than my doubts
What I'm trying to say
I mean what I'm saying is
You love
What I hate
About myself
I wanted to believe
You were my next mistake
But I was mistaken
Moment by moment
We grow another inch
Moving forward, slowly
The new normal is you
Parking lot conversations
Roses are red
Violets are blue
This confession
Is inspired by you...

My Happy Poem

My surroundings have been dark
Life has shown me its ugliness
Most of my words dance on painful floors
That's where my truth sings the loudest
But I've experienced happy feet
Moving to tunes that inspire my pride
Every time my words transform into poems
I shout on the inside
Jumping up and down
Because God did it again
Another scale has shredded
A new layer of skin has been found
Thank You Jesus
For the joy, You give
In spite of my sins
Testimonies inspire my emptiness
No longer am I alone
Freedom of the unknown brings peace
Happy feet tingle again
To a secret place
That explains my fate
A seductive cage engulfed in words
Pain, passion and pleasure
Outline my emotions
This mystery leads me to happy.

Love

I fantasize about you in my sleep
Hoping for a chance to become familiar with your beauty
Yearning for you to touch my soul
Imprint your signature on every inch of my body
The thought causes my breathing to become irregular

Wait—
Let me open my eyes
I don't want this steam
To corrupt my vision
Maybe I'm dreaming
I've never felt such sensation
The hairs on my skin are excited
My pores are climaxing off your presence
This must be an introduction to heaven
The sun is shining bright
My mind is turned on
The birds are playing with the bees
But no one is hurting
How could this be
I've never experienced such energy
Life being lived abundantly
Tears have no posture to exist
If only you had a frame to kiss
Some think I'm crazy
For speaking about you in such a tone
But I've been without you for too long
Love
Thank you for your intimacy
You will always be my friend
But forgive me in advance
If my heart doesn't always
Want to hold your hand.

Heart Angel

If I had to pick a word
I'd say unexpected
Out of nowhere
The wind blew her
In my direction
An insecure place
Secure with being alone
Protecting what's left
Which wasn't much
Tired of being
What they need
Leaving me empty
And forgetting about me
Filling me with hope
That left me hopeless
Until she showed up
A real woman
Fragile and warm
The missing piece
I was unaware of
Taking time to out love
My Flaws
Things I hated
About myself
Real wealth
Her heart was my help
I was persuaded
To find me
Not the shallow version
But the little Giant
The open wound
Heart made of pain
Clearing out the clutter
In Jesus name
It's okay to cry
Feel what you feel
Is she for real?
I thought I was dreaming
But there she was
All the time
Even when it was hard

Weak but strong
She had my back
When my back had no bone
Had my side when I was bent
No money in my pocket
Just years of lint
What does she want?
I don't have much
"Soften your heart," she said
Let go of your perceptions
I'm not out to get you
Just allow us to be
This love
I've never known
Spiritual connection
Nothing else can explain it
Hard to comprehend
A friend that's friendlier
Than most
In a bad way
I mean
A good way
That's bad
Bold and beautiful

Wait—
I'm tripping
To say she's beautiful
Is an insult
She can't be categorized
Defined or replaced
This heart angel
Saved my life
By loving me right.

Just My Imagination

I see eagles
Soaring beyond the clouds
Preparing the way
Tickling my doubt
I'm laughing
At the enemy
He thought he had me
It's running away
Who?
My imagination
I hear music
This sound
Has loosed shackles
Tied around my ankles
I'm moving fast
Smiling with the sun
Living life
Like there's only one
It's running away
Who?
My imagination
I feel redemption
This liberation
Has granted me wisdom
Sucking into those dry places
That wanted to die
Smoking on the spirit within
High on purpose
Craving a dream
That already came true
It's running away
Who?
My imagination
I taste future
This flavor embodies my attention
Sweet and sour
A tangy combination
Believing in the unseen
Teasing my ambition
It's running away
Who?

My imagination
I smell success
Around the corner
Waiting to congratulate
My patience
The grounds are solid
Sturdy and faithful
Every mistake
Has validated its purpose
It's running away
Who?
Me
Imaginations do become
Reality.

Key West

As the sun sets
We reflect on past and future destinations
Rocky roads challenge our commitment
The climb tests our endurance
But at the top of our mountains
There's a light
Not just any light
But the kind that fights
To make its presence known
Standing tall on bending knees
Trusting God with what feels perfect
And unsure at the same time
Our minds are constantly under attack
Searching for missing pieces
Trying to make sense
Out of chaos and confusion
Only to realize
What we're seeking
Is within the darkness
Hidden inside ourselves
It is in the valley
That we walk side by side with our shadows
Just like the hero
At the end of a good movie
We'll get through this
Because we're SUPERDUVEE!

Single Mother

Today is a day
Mothers all over the world
Celebrate the gift of life
And all are reminded of this selfless sacrifice.

It's an honor
To say you've experienced
Such a blessing
That gives an instant heart connection that can't be explained.

Although we don't always get it right
We do the best we can with what we know
And pray that God will help us along the way.

I know what it's like to anticipate a better life
Yet darkness steals your dreams
And often you can't see
That light at the end of the tunnel.

The reality is that life isn't fair
And the only one to depend on is God.

I wanted you to know
That you're a strong woman
A woman who can stand
Even when she feels like falling.

You're bigger than your failures or the pain
You're a woman who has a lot to win and so much to gain.

When your back is against that wall
And you don't know what else to do, pray your way through.

Talk to God and know that He is the definition of a real lover
Just like the bond you have created
By being a single mother.

Mama

Today we celebrate you
But I want to reflect on those years
You took me under your wings.

Don't ever think for one second
That I don't remember the sacrifices
You made for me.

If it hadn't been for you
Life could have easily passed me by.

There's a lot of things I didn't understand
But I never questioned your loyalty
For making sure
I had food in my mouth and clothes on my back.

You did the best you could
With what you had, and today
I boldly say...Thank you!

Mama, you didn't know this
But I needed you more than
My expressions could show.

I appreciate the time you invested in me
Those dresses (I didn't like) you took the time to make
And most importantly
Placing me in an environment
That required me to be in church on Sunday mornings and nights.

I know that you may have been disappointed in me
Because I was not the ideal example of a grandchild
But know that God has always had His hand on me.

One day you will understand my defaults in life
But today is your day
So, enjoy and grow in God's love.

I love you, Grandma Rena!

Because of Me

Because of me
You saw an image
That sparked interest

Because of me
You desired
The unknown

Because of me
You smiled more
Throughout the day

Because of me
You had faith
Not to make mistakes

Because of me
You tried to
let the past go

Because of me
You opened
A closed door

Because of me
You felt safe
Almost untouchable

Because of me
You needed
A calmer life

Because of me
You looked
In reality's mirror

Because of me
You wanted
To be loved
But now...

Because of me
You want to forget
What made your heart beat

Because of me
You breathe air
polluted with grief

Because of me
You fight
The desire

Because of me
You feel
Stupid and unappreciated

Because of me
You can't
Balance respect

Because of me
You Cry
With closed eyes

Because of me
You identify with
Shameful insecurities

Because of me
You have
Regrets

Because of me
You don't
Believe in the dream

Because of us
You and me
Can't be.

Mr. Perry

You are the voice
That Inspires
People like me
To have faith
In an unfulfilled dream
Because your story lives
It defines divine purpose
Your journey
Was an experience
For
The least
The left out
The broken hearted
The abused
The confused
The dreamer
The one who has God's favor
Many are called
But only a few
Are actually chosen
I love you
But I fell in love
With your story
To witness your success
Is to be reminded
That God is faithful
And He does everything
He promises
Your childhood
Was a cross
You had to bear
So that millions
Would believe
That God is still able
The test is unfair at times
And the price seems
Too high to pay
But ordered steps
Have to follow
His way
He knows what He's doing

Thanks for the testimony
You are the voice
That Inspires
People like me
To one day
Change the world like you!

Love Chronicles

You fell in love with a distraction
Not real love but you call it that
So, you'll never have to look back
At the one who really had your heart
But tore it apart...
#love

Here's my heart
If you break it
Don't worry
Just promise
You'll be able
To put it
Back together...
#love

How many hearts
Do we break
To realize
You and me
Are meant
To be...
#love

I'm not asking
For you to protect
My heart
Just treat it
As if
It were
Your own.
#love

What if you were
Making me all
I was meant to be
In order for someone
Else to experience
Being happy...
#love

Please don't rain
On my parade
Even if it isn't true
Let me believe
One day
I'll be with
You...
#love

I couldn't
Love you
Until I
Hated pride
By then
It was too late
The greatest X
Escaped...
#love

We used to like
Each other
Before we started
Loving each other...
#love

Time flies when
You're around
Make it stop...
#love

A lot of people
Are reaping the heartache of seeds
Sown by someone else's emotional crimes.
#love

I waited for you
As long as I could
You never showed
So I left...
#love

Roses are red
Violets are blue
I would love to spend
My forever with you.
#love

I just wanted
To know
What it's like
To want each other
At the same time...
#love

Hide and seek
There you go again
Playing around
In my mind
Timeout...
Be my Valentines.
#love

Walking backwards
To an empty table
Taking a seat
When your heart
Reminds you
You'll never
Get a full meal
To eat
And still, you stay
Hoping for one day...
#love

The Refinery

Psalm 119:71 (KJV)

It is good for me that I have been afflicted; that I might learn thy statutes.

There's a stain
On my heart
Signed by you
Felt inside of me
I'm trying
To scrub it away
Manually
But
It's too dark
Fifty shades of dirty
Must clean
Spiritually.

Little Giant

You left me
In the deep
On purpose
Forced me
To swim
Against the tide
You knew
I could handle
The waves
All those times
I thought I was going to die
You were right there
Holding me on both sides
I'm here today
Only because of Your grace
Compacted inspiration
Ready to encourage nations
All because You trusted me
When I couldn't trust myself
One day at a time
This Little giant
Has a victorious mind.

#TBH

I stand boldly yet humble
In Your presence
Confessing the obvious
I've prayed prayers not for answers
Simply protocol
It sounds good to rebuke sin
Make it flee
But I asked myself
Did I really mean
What I just said?
No
There are sins
I want to stay
So why pray for them to go away
Many won't understand such truth
But You do
You're not surprised
It's one of the reasons
You hung your head
And died.

Do You Know…

What it feels like
To be a saint and sinner
Off track like time
Going back an hour
The devil and Jesus
Fighting for one's attention
When the battle ends
A wounded Christian
For the world to see
Pretending life is great
Allergic to mistakes
Perfection has taken over
Hanging with a higher power
You have become
The perfect liar
Invisible hypocrite
The biggest one
On planet earth
Behind closed doors
Your life is a circus
In the face of many
Born again flesh
Sexing sin daily
Bondage is your color
The devil and Jesus
Intimate lovers
Humping your conscience
Ready to claim victory
Over your life
Forced to tell the truth
Afraid of your next move
Shame the devil
Live in your truth
A form of dust
Saved sinner who trusts
The cross
His blood
An unconditional love
Too great to comprehend
The one who saved you
Has this world in His hands

So never pretend
To impress people
Who are just like you
You'll lose your way
Blinding the spirit
Heartless Christians
Don't want to be equal
With Honesty
Image is a slave
They can't keep it real
But a pure heart
Will get you in the gates
In class until death
Perfect through His eyes
Never our own
Sinning doesn't end
He fixes what's broken
Fighting to be one's focus
Life was planned before you were born
The enemy came to kill, steal and destroy
Pray for spiritual twins
Mercy and grace
They'll protect you
From hurt, harm and danger
But Jesus can't be a stranger
In your life
There is no one
Powerful enough
To take His place
This is a saved sinner
Thankful for grace.

Spiritual Death

Like the grains of sand by the sea
My sins are plenty
Every time we get a chance
A seductive dance is displayed
Lustful
Spending unforgettable pointless moments together
Walking hand in hand
Leaving the dance floor empty
Temporary fix is my drug of choice
Confused
It plays on my intelligence
My prayers are interrupted
I feel like the devil's advocate
Getting comfortable doing things my own way
Faithless
Trying to cure my self-inflicted injuries
Manipulating the outside
In order to hide the pain on the inside
Hopeful
God you're the only thing I haven't tried
Take control over this broken vessel
I can't take another empty step
I don't want to make another move without You
Please hear this confession
Take off the blinders
Help me to see nothing else, accept Your will for my life
Spiritual death is not my name
Take me to your cross
Validate me with Your pain.

He Loves You

Have you ever seen
A happy face
Broken on the inside
Look in the mirror
But close your eyes
Concentrate on the darkness
Become one with the silence
Look at all the stuff
You can't bring outside
The surface is a hero
Internally, the cape has lost its power
Nobody knows
That your soul has died
You're living off of false air
Nobody wise enough to care
The truth hasn't discovered you
Bondage owns your life
A constant fight
With no gloves
The only thing protecting you
Is God's love.

We're A Consequence

Adam and Eve
Reaping what they've sown
We did not create sin
It was already here
Waiting to manipulate us
Universal, yet complex
An addiction
We're suppose to hate
But we don't
So conviction
Turns into pride
My sin isn't as bad as yours
And yours is worse than mine
We conveniently waste time
On pointless chatter
Fifty shades of lies
Dumbfounded by the One
Who forgives
Guilt and shame says
Our sinful nature is unworthy
But Jesus says
Mercy and grace can't be replaced
So stop rejecting My love
Ask ME for help
The cross is where I died
So that you could live
The grave is where they buried Me
But it wasn't My home
In three days
I was consumed with power
To forgive
The things you've done wrong.

Revelation

I've collected weeds
Dark and ugly truths
Caressing my conscience
Making me wiser
I've been broken
To be put back together
Better with pain
Regaining self-delight
Private victories
All of it has gotten me
To this place
Right now
Grateful
Ready for new mistakes
Stronger wisdom
More let downs
Bigger dreams
No longer a slave
To uncomfortable days.

I See You

Stop. Breathe. Slow down.

You're tired
It's lonely and cold
You're shaking
Scared of living empty
You feel hopeless
Stop. Breathe. Slow down.

I see you

They're a distraction
You trust them
More than Me
Even when their pain
Brings you to your knees
Stop. Breathe. Slow down.

I see you

But you won't see Me
I'm here waiting
You've done it your way
Now it's My turn
Your load is too heavy
Let Me carry your burdens
Not with judgment, but compassion
Take off your worries
Place them at My feet
He/she won't satisfy you anymore
They were a band-aid
Incapable of healing
What I allowed to break
Naked is how I need you
It's the only way
I the Father, Son and Holy Ghost
Can help you
Remember…

I see you.

Dear God...

We're tired of praying prayers that have no faith
You know us better than we know ourselves
So why do we constantly try to play on Your intelligence?

It's so disrespectful how we carry on from day to day
Without telling You 'thank You'
We don't make the time to talk to You
Because our thoughts are polluted
With guilt and muzzled by shame
Forgive us!

Not only do we ask for forgiveness
But help us to do better
With our relationship with you God.

Make us put the same efforts
That we put into our personal relationships
Into our spiritual walk with You.

We can't do it without you God!

Most of us want to be closer to You
But we're afraid of change
We're afraid that walking with You
Is going to require too much.

We're not worthy God
We don't even have enough sense
To comprehend that You love us
Even when we don't love ourselves.

You bless us because You are God
And not always based on our behaviors.

God shows us the way
Help us to know You for ourselves
And not how people feel we should know You.

We're ready for a new beginning
It is in Your name we pray...Amen!

Spirit and Truth

Every time the doors open
I'm there
Standing amongst
A camouflaged congregation
Giving God the highest praise
My Hallelujah
Belongs to You
Ignoring the lows
Wearing a smile
To impress
The onlookers
Once the makeup has worn off
Holy and righteousness gets lost
Broken sinners
You will never see
The crowd is too full of pride
We're not allowed to be honest
Pretending is a new religion
The essence of God's love
Invisible
It's been rewired and tainted
By confused people
Who want God
To have human instinct
Selfish and unconditional
No compassion and judgmental
Inspired by
Who can memorize
The most Bible verses
You can find me
In church
Hands raised
Heart open
Anticipating a word
From God
You see last night
I wasn't so faithful
As a matter of fact
I'm unfaithful daily
There's is always something
Ungodly about my behavior

I've learned that there's liberty
In being honest with God
I'm not claiming to be perfect
I need Him each and every day
How I behave
Doesn't compare
To my level of praise
You see
I'm not worthy
Shouldn't be blessed
Got years' worth of mess
But it won't stop me
From giving God glory
I won't pretend
Everything is perfect
Through God
I am made whole
Don't allow camouflaged Christians
To mold you into their breed
Be who you are
God can work wonders with an honest heart!

It's You

Father God we come saying thank You
Thank You for peace
Thank You for keeping us
From dangers seen and unseen God
You are so faithful
We don't deserve any of Your grace or mercy
But because You are God
And You have a purpose for our lives
You keep keeping us
God, sometimes we don't have the words to say
At times we don't even know what to pray
But we ask you to read our hearts
Show us the way
Not only the way
But Your ways God
We need You like never before
We want a different encounter with You God
Give us the wisdom
To understand people and things around us
We know we're not perfect
But we have to be better
Get us focused on You
And less of ourselves
There's nobody that can do the things
You have and will do in our lives
We don't want to settle anymore God
Awaken our drive and desire for You God
Let us get more than just a word
But a new attitude about life
And the call You've trusted us to have
Protect our families, friends and every person
We've ever known
Help us to respect one another
Give us patience and compassion
It is in Jesus name we pray
Amen!

In Spite Of

Every time I turn around
A leech is sucking me dry
Weighing on my emotions
Grabbing me by the ankles
Twisting my stability
Unable to walk a straight line
Pulled in the past
Reminded of the pain
Blinded by the shame
Living in sin
Generation after generation
Be quiet
Nobody has to know
Crippling my growth
Denial lurks within
Covering the heart
With manipulation
Unable to care
Racist to love
Until...
God showed me His hand
He took my faults
Hid them behind the cross
He gave His Son
Who died
For me to live
Through His name
I've been redeemed
There's a faithful ending
Every failure conquered
Brings Him glory
I'm able to tell the story
About a name above any other name
I'm able to encourage
Because of the shame
I'm able to love
In spite of the pain.

Insomnia Prayer

It's 3:47 am
I can't sleep
My posture won't rest
A confession needs to be released
We talk all the time
But
I haven't been honest with my words
Maybe it's pain or the struggle
Let me stop
It's...
An unsatisfyingly satisfying comfort that haunts me
Day in and day out
Tired literally lives in the lining of my mouth
Everybody always has something to say
Truth and fiction sound the same
But...
I believe in You
Your words are true
The love
You display is uncomprehending
It's mind boggling
I just wish You didn't
Trust me so much
My profile picture for life
Rotates in Your mercy and grace daily
Filthy describes my holy temple
Disrespect is how I respect Your vessel
Don't use me to encourage Your people
I'm not worthy of the praise
Nor the undeserved accolades
You sit high
Look low
Then there's me
Standing in the need
Of what you ask
Nobody knows but You
Again
I had all the answers
When You weren't asking me a question
I feel a wave
Up and down

Tug of war
In the left corner
We have a bold devil
In the right corner
We have a mighty God
In the middle
Me...
Standing alone
Pleading for my life
Don't let him get me Jesus!
This battle isn't mine
So why do I feel like I'm fighting?
I'm weak
Don't tell society because they'll preach
You're strong
Tackle those demons
Stomp on the devil's head
Resist temptation
Pray
Read to show thyself approved
Fast
Consecrate yourself
Don't do this or that
Change your mindset
Have faith
Believe
Feed your spirit
Act like it's already done
These remedies are for the victory
But...
I still waver from time to time
Can I be honest?
At times I don't want to be kept
It's temporary satisfaction
I know
Aggravation is my consequence
The love I can see is what my flesh desires
Falling is my repercussion
Saved
But...
Too selfish to completely humble myself
In Your authority.

New Birth

When I was released from my mother's womb
All my rights remained within the umbilical cord
Life was unknown
This sinful world could only identify with me through
The classifications of a name
No being but God
Could comprehend the destiny
Created for a chosen child
Or see the ministry within a burdened soul.

My name had no definition until life unraveled
And trust became foreign.
Innocence no longer attached itself to my skin
I was given the responsibility to recreate my original identity,
Which was lost in the lines of parental communications.

Of course, I didn't realize this until my adult life
But like I said before, I was a chosen child
Meaning that my life could not be my own
Pain, rejection, neglect, heartache and disappointments
Would all play a significant role that taunted me from time to time.

Those dark days yearn for darker nights
Every living thing seemed to be living in vain
Self-defeat had taken my created identity
Forcing me to pledge for another disguise
But I was tired
I couldn't take any more of what the world had to offer.

If I wasn't broken, how could I have been fixed?
If I had no shame
My destiny would have no fame
Or glory for that Name
That conquers above any other names.

Spiritually Bipolar

To see my life
Is to witness
The power of God's favor.

To hear my words
Is to be inspired
By wisdom.

To touch my heart
Is to feel my wounds in the flesh.

To taste my thoughts
Is to be filled
With the complexities of my faith.

To smell my desires
Is to be confused by the enemy.

These are the senses of my spirituality.

Mister Man

My silence is broken
Everybody knows
What you did to me
I've been on display for years
The curtains couldn't handle
All those partials scaling from my skeletons
It was an invisible tattoo
That created multiple layers of denial, confusion and judgment
One error after another
Connecting me to dots that leave holes in my heart
I allowed your malfunctions
To scar my moments with darkness
Pain learned how to suppress itself for years
Until emptiness took over the tears
I didn't know who I was because
You were who you are
I knew you weren't supposed to touch me
But in some sick way, you made me believe
That it was ok for my body to gain this type of attention
My nose is burning, and my eyes are filling up with water
For I know that at this very moment
This is happening to someone's daughter
Hating you was a part of my plan
But God didn't allow you to mess up
My entire self-worth with the manipulation of your hands
I bet you didn't know that you were chosen just like me
You see, God knew all this would happen
But He also knew that these circumstances
Would produce a voice within my soul
You see, I'm chosen for greatness
You...you were chosen as an instrument
To disrespect my innocence
It was a process that had to be birthed
In order for my words to grow into a story
That would command the attention of nations
I didn't know who I was until
You did what you were supposed to do
Mister man I say thank you!

Torn. Lost. Confused.

Life ain't fair but neither is favor
You love God but...
The world is easier on the eyes
It's a battle within the mind
A war that competes for your attention daily
You're tired of being tired
Looking for a way out
Desperate for change
Your loyalty lies with pain
You can hear His name but...
Paperback Christians with religious appeal
Keep you feeling worthless, hopeless and discouraged
Convictions jail your heart
White walls are all you see
Every direction is the wrong way
No oxygen to believe in your own prayers
Sins are too dirty
To plant infected seeds
Would be destructive
Like a lifeless child
You dare to dream
Afraid of the possibilities
On the inside
You have a desire to do right but...
Selfishness craves the wrong appetites
What can He do with somebody like you
Now you're more confused
Running from a future
That gets better in time
All for the sake of people
As I write these words
I release freedom
The atmosphere is too toxic
Hurt people are hurting people
I know what it's like
To love God
And like the world a lot
People won't allow us to be honest but...
God respects our humility
He works it out for our good
It's a mindset

If you believe you're a failure
then you will be a failure but...
You're not a failure
That's what the enemy wants you to think
You're more than a conqueror
The Creator is your Father
There's nothing too hard for Him
He has all power but...
You must be willing
To remove any form of negative energy
He's not the Author of confusion
Unconditional love is His specialty but...
He won't wait forever
Find out about God for yourself
Don't allow people to snatch your purpose
He's faithful every day
Don't make Him any promises you can't keep
Just pray and stay at His feet
I'm telling you what I know
Not something I heard
Always remember to stay in the will of God
Continually asking for forgiveness
Because the world is unfaithfully dying
If you fall down
Get back up and keep trying
You see I'm no different from you
Yet He has gifted me the opportunity to inspire you!

Unseen

When I dream
I see a version of me
That does not yet exist
It's like a seed waiting
On nature to take its course
And like a thief in the night
The enemy taunts me
With his voice
"It won't happen, you can't do it,
you don't have enough money,
you've done too many bad things,
God couldn't possibly be that unconditional
to bless you
with what you've seen
in a dream."

But the devil is a liar!

Dreamer dream on
God will take you higher
In time
Just keep purpose
In the forefront of your mind.

Orphan

There is no mercy found in complaints
Darkness does not hide me
My heart is beaming with radiant insecurities
I laugh to avoid crying
If the truth was told
I have nobody to hold my hand or my heart
The world I reside in has me dependent on my fears
I lean toward my shadow for consolation
There's no parental concern in my home
And the unknown wants me to adjust with being alone
It's a daily ritual for me to suppress these demons
Nobody even notices that life's emptiness is drowning me
If I can make a smile laugh, my job has been done
And another day has gone by without me fixing my hidden problems
It's not easy being a pretender, you always have to keep a straight face
No room for mistakes
Your ability to believe in another human being
Sounds tempting
But the disappointment
Is just too heavy to lift
I heard about a Man named Jesus
They say He's a burden barrier
A mind regulator, a heart fixer,
A mother to the motherless and a father to the fatherless
So surely, He has the power to transform tribulations
Faith wants us to confess
God will do the rest!

Black Boy Magic

When you think of me
Embrace the struggle
Bring truth to power
We have not overcome
A new son just a different day
We are free, but not mentally
Our environments are hopeless
We're too hungry to focus
On a way out
Surviving is our priority
It's hard to trust a system
Designed for you to fail
We have few options
Death or jail
Being Black is a weapon
Of mass destruction
If only we knew
Our royal truth
We can't breathe
So why are we
Their enemy?
Can't you see
What poverty and lack
Is doing to us?
No, we're not perfect
But we don't deserve this
We are being killed
Sometimes by our own people
And those who make us feel unequal
Famed by our deaths
We need you
To be our voice
Not on a shirt
But through positive demonstration
Let the world know
A change has to come
Black magic stand up
And rescue your sons
Or we will continue
To die by the gun
Inspired by a Black male on the run!

In Closing...

It is my prayer that, in sharing these parts of me – my thoughts, emotions, convictions, hurts, pains, joys, challenges, triumphs, disappointments, guilt, shame, faith and journey through life, I've helped you find comfort and solace in your sorrows; inspired a breakthrough and change of heart and mind.

Even when the journey feels unbearable or overwhelming, embrace it. Don't pretend to be too strong or ignore it like it doesn't exist. This is one of our *biggest* problems. Although it's going to hurt – it's part of the process to healing.

If you've been encouraged in any way - pass this diary on! God gave me the courage to expose the pieces of me that caused my soul to bleed so that you can go forth and be free.

Shanteria "The Little Giant" Griglen

www.ingramcontent.com/pod-product-compliance
Lightning Source LLC
LaVergne TN
LVHW011208080426
835508LV00007B/665